MW00834527

101 Things to Do in

ALABAMA

Before You Up and Die

SWEET
WATER
PRESS

101 Things to Do in Alabama
Copyright © 2006 Sweetwater Press
Produced by Cliff Road Books

All rights reserved. No part of this book may be reproduced by any means whatsoever, neither mechanical, electronic, nor digital, without written permission from the publisher, except brief excerpts quoted for purpose of review.

ISBN: 1-58173-555-3
ISBN-13: 9781581735550

Researched and co-written by Holly Smith
Jacket and text design by Miles G. Parsons
Printed in Italy

1. Climb to the top of Mt. Cheaha.

2. Eat fried green
tomatoes.

yes

3. Call someone
"hon."

yes

4. Drink sweet tea *yes* from morning 'til night.

5. Canoe the Cahaba.

6. Save a Cahaba Lily.

7. Tip a cow. *yes*

8. Catch beads at Mardi Gras in Mobile.

9. Throw beads at Mardi Gras in Mobile.

10. See a UFO on *yes* Sand Mountain.

11. Help a hurricane survivor.

yes

12. Go to a church
supper on the
grounds.

13. Sing sacred harp. *yes*

❧

14. Take in the view from Vulcan. *yes*

15. Have your picture taken with the boll weevil monument in Enterprise.

16. Visit the ghost of Sloss Furnaces on Halloween.

17. Toss a mullet at the Flora-Bama.

18. Cruise the Alabama River on a riverboat.

yes

19. Catch a roll at Lambert's.

20. Plant a ^yes redbud tree.

21. Listen to the mockingbirds in Monroeville.

22. Hike the Sipsey Wilderness.

23. Eat peaches *yes* every which way you can.

24. Visit the peach water tower in Clanton while eating peaches every which way you can.

yes

25. Deep fry a turkey. (Or just deep fry something.)

26. Camp out on the infield at Talladega Superspeedway.

27. Watch the sunset from the Pink Pony.

28. Kayak the Locust Fork River.

29. Climb a
Mississippian
Indian mound.

30. Say a prayer at Hank Williams' grave.

31. Shake a leg at the W.C. Handy Music Festival.

32. Meet the celebrity of the month at the Alabama Music Hall of Fame.

33. Visit the first
White House of the
Confederacy.

yes

34. Decorate your *yes* whole neighborhood with Christmas lights. The more the better.

35. Buy a used car from a minor local celebrity.

36. Have your picture taken in front of Dexter Avenue Baptist Church.

yes

37. Master the art
of the banana
puddin'.

yes

38. Take off for the U.S. Space and Rocket Center.

yes

39. Take a dolphin cruise.

40. Sight a bald eagle over Lake Guntersville.

41. Go to the Dismals (so you can say you did).

42. See the azaleas at Bellingrath Gardens in spring.

43. Visit the sea lions at the Birmingham Zoo.

yes

44. Eat a bag of boiled peanuts.

yes

45. Bundle up for Christmas on the River in Demopolis.

46. Golf the Robert Trent Jones trail.

47. Ride in the hot-air balloon festival in Decatur.

yes

48. Get your hair
done at a good
old-fashioned
beauty parlor.

49. Take off on Rampage at Visionland.

50. Play medieval games at the Alabama Renaissance Faire in Florence.

51. Meet the band
Alabama on
Fan Day in
Fort Payne.

yes

52. Shout your head off at a Huntsville Havoc hockey game.

yes

53. Take in an IMAX movie at the McWane Center.

54. See the battlefields at Horseshoe Bend. *yes*

55. Visit the pits at the Birmingham International Raceway.

56. Go at least once to the Alabama Shakespeare Festival.

57. Go horseback riding along the Tennessee River.

58. Pan for gold.

59. Walk across the
footbridge to
Noccalula Falls.

60. Do the caverns: Rickwood, DeSoto, and Cathedral!

61. Take your mama to lunch at the Bright Star.

yes

62. Hear the Alabama Symphony in concert.

63. Watch a classic movie and hear the Mighty Wurlitzer at the Alabama Theatre.

yes

64. Go skiing in Mentone.

65. Munch on *yes* samples at Priester's Pecans.

66. Marvel at *yes* Ave Maria Grotto in Cullman.

67. Join a volunteer fire department.

68. Browse through the 450-mile yard sale.

69. Attend *yes* Christmas in the Country at Homestead Hollow.

70. Pick pumpkins *yes* at a pumpkin patch.

yes

71. Get lost in a corn maze.

72. Find a treasure at Tannehill Trade Days.

yes

yes

73. Tailgate at the
Iron Bowl.

yes

74. Shop 'til you
drop in
Birmingham.

75. Take flight in a simulator at the Southern Museum of Flight.

76. Get on Rick 'n' Bubba.

yes

77. Catch lightning bugs.

78. Lie in the grass *yes* watching a meteor shower.

79. Waterski at Smith Lake in September.

80. Spend an entire summer day at the ballpark.

81. Write a song about a dog, your mama, your sweetheart, or jail.

yes

82. Sit in a rocking chair on a porch and do nothing.

83. Go to a race at Barber Motorsports Park.

84. Eat ribs at the original Dreamland.

85. Learn to country dance.

86. Ride the Fort Morgan ferry.

yes

87. Hop aboard the USS <u>Alabama</u>.

88. See at least one gator up close and personal.

yes

~

89. Shop at an outlet mall.

yes

90. Get Alabama *yes* red clay all over your shoes.

91. Get bitten by a chigger. *yes*

92. Try some homemade muscadine wine.

93. Walk across a covered bridge.

94. Sail the Tennessee-Tombigbee Waterway.

yes

95. Cross the
Edmund Pettus
Bridge in Selma.

96. Relive Winston County's secession from the Confederacy at Looney's Tavern Amphitheater.

97. Tour Arlington and Gaineswood antebellum homes.

98. Go bass fishing. yes

99. Attend the
Governor's
Inaugural Parade.

yes

100. Call a turkey.

yes

101. Stand under a
dogwood in spring
and be glad.
You're in Alabama!